MOSQUITO-BORNE ILLNESSES

MOSQUITO-BORNE ILLNESSES

Kristi Lew

Marshall Cavendish
Benchmark
New York

Special thanks to Raymond J. Dattwyler, MD, Professor of Medicine and Microbiology/Immunology at New York Medical College, for his expert review of the manuscript.

Marshall Cavendish Benchmark
99 White Plains Road
Tarrytown, New York 10591-5502
www.marshallcavendish.us

This book is not intended for use as a substitute for advice, consultation, or treatment by a licensed medical practitioner. The reader is advised that no action of a medical nature should be taken without consultation with a licensed medical practitioner, including action that may seem to be indicated by the contents of this work, since individual circumstances vary and medical standards, knowledge, and practices change with time. The publisher, author, and medical consultants disclaim all liability and cannot be held responsible for any problems that may arise from the use of this book.

Library of Congress Cataloging-in-Publication Data
Lew, Kristi.
Mosquito-borne illnesses / by Kristi Lew.
p. cm. — (Health alert)
Includes index.
Summary: "Provides comprehensive information on the causes, treatment, and history of mosquito-borne illnesses"—Provided by publisher.
ISBN 978-0-7614-3980-6
,1. West Nile fever—Juvenile literature. I. Title.
RA644.W47L49 2010
614.4'323—dc22

2008051013

Front Cover: A female mosquito as seen under a microscope.

Photo research by Candlepants Incorporated
Cover Photo: Phototake Inc. / Alamy Images

The photographs in this book are used by permission and through the courtesy of:
Getty Images: WIN-Initiative, 2; Richard Pasley - Doctor Stock, 7; Science VU/CDC, 13; 3D4Medical.com, 14; Tyler Stableford / Aurora Outdoor Collection, 17; Rick Poley, 19; 29, 34, 40; Steve Gorton, 31; Gary John Norman, 36; Nucleus Medical Art, Inc., 44; Peter Ginter, 47; Joedson Alves/AFP, 49; David Roth, 53; Christopher Drake, 55. *Alamy Images*: blickwinkel, 5, 18; imagebroker, 9; Kay Blaschke, 10; Arni Katz, 21; Peter Arnold, Inc., 24; Glasshouse Images, 32. *Corbis*: Visuals Unlimited, 26.

Editor: Joy Bean
Publisher: Michelle Bisson
Art Director: Anahid Hamparian

Printed in Malaysia

6 5 4 3 2 1

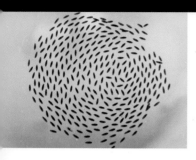

CONTENTS

[1]

WHAT IS IT LIKE TO HAVE A MOSQUITO-BORNE ILLNESS?

Emma feels terrible. She is stuck indoors and bundled up under a blanket while her friends are outside playing on one of the last summer days before school starts again. "Getting sick in the wintertime is bad," Emma thinks, "but being sick during the summer is even worse."

Emma has been dozing on and off all day. Her whole body aches, especially her head. Her back and neck feel stiff, too. And even though it is hot outside, she wrapped herself in a blanket because she felt so cold that she was shivering. As soon as she got under the blanket, however, she started to sweat. No matter how hard she tries, she just cannot get comfortable.

Emma's mother takes her temperature and tells Emma that she has a fever. When someone has a fever, it means that his or

A fever is one of the first signs of many illnesses, including some mosquito-borne illnesses.

her body temperature is warmer than normal. A normal body temperature for most people is around 98.6 degrees Fahrenheit (37 degrees Celsius). When germs such as **viruses**, **bacteria**, and **parasites** enter the body, they can make you sick. One of the ways the body defends itself against these invaders is to turn up the heat.

Emma's mother also feels her daughter's neck and finds two hard, swollen lumps on either side of her throat. These lumps are Emma's lymph glands, or **lymph nodes**. These nodes are a part of the body's **immune system**. The immune system's job is to fight invading germs. When the body is fighting an infection, the lymph nodes sometimes swell in reaction.

Emma's mom is concerned about Emma's fever and other **symptoms**. It looks as if Emma might have the flu, but it seems strange for her to get the flu in August. Most people catch the flu virus in the wintertime. Emma's mom wonders if there are other illnesses that have the same symptoms. To ease her mind, she decides to take Emma to the doctor.

At the doctor's office, Emma has an examination. Her doctor agrees that Emma appears to have flu-like symptoms and that her mother made the right decision by bringing Emma in to the doctor's office. The doctor also notices that Emma has a rash on her stomach and back. The doctor asks Emma and her mother if they have taken any trips to foreign countries lately. They tell the doctor that they have not.

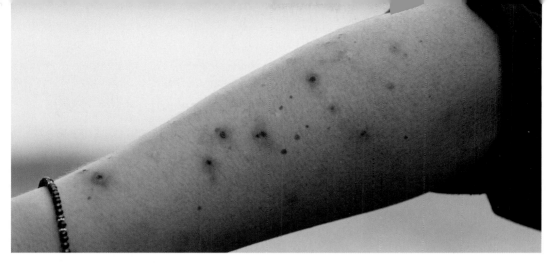

Most mosquito bites do not lead to mosquito-borne illnesses.

The doctor also asks them if Emma could have been bitten by a mosquito recently. Emma thinks back to last weekend, when her family had a backyard cookout. There were lots of mosquitoes around during the cookout, especially as the sun started to go down. Emma hates getting bitten by mosquitoes. They make her itch and break out in big red welts. She always tries to spray herself with insect repellent. But now she remembers that she and her friends were playing around the lake in her backyard, and she forgot to reapply the spray. After the cookout, she was covered in red, itchy bumps. But then they stopped itching and went away. Emma tells her doctor about her mosquito bites from last weekend.

Based on Emma's symptoms and recent mosquito bites, the doctor suspects that Emma has an illness caused by the West Nile virus (WNV). When someone gets bitten by a mosquito infected with the virus, the person can get sick. The doctor tells Emma and her mother that a number of people in their community have come to the doctor's office with fevers this summer, and their blood tested positive for traces of the West Nile virus. The doctor is not yet certain that Emma has the West Nile virus. The only way to be sure is to send some of Emma's blood to a laboratory so it can be tested. Emma will have to wait a few days for the test results.

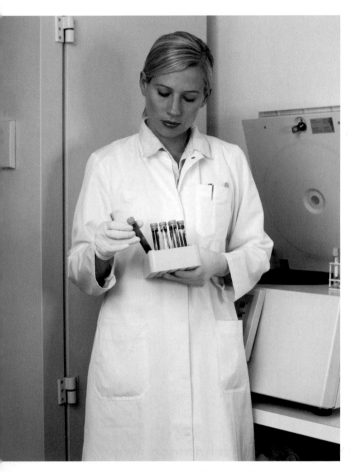

The only way to find out if you have a mosquito-borne illness is to have your blood tested in a laboratory.

Emma asks the doctor if she has to get a shot. Even if a shot would make her feel better, she would rather not have one. The doctor replies that she has no medicine to treat West Nile fever. Emma's illness will just have to run its course and go away by itself.

Emma is relieved that she doesn't need a shot, but she wants to know if she has to miss the first day of school next week. She is looking forward to seeing her friends on their first day in middle school. Emma's doctor assures her that, most likely, Emma will be well enough to attend the first day of school—symptoms caused by the West Nile virus usually go away in a few days.

Emma's mother wants to know if the other kids at Emma's school can catch West Nile virus from Emma. In other words, is the West Nile virus **contagious**? The doctor tells Emma's mother that Emma's friends and teachers will be perfectly safe. The virus cannot be passed from person to person like a cold or the flu. It can only be transmitted by the bite of an infected mosquito.

However, Emma's doctor cautions, the West Nile virus can sometimes cause symptoms that are much worse than Emma's. If her temperature continues to rise, or if her headache becomes much worse, that might mean she could develop a severe condition called West Nile **encephalitis**. Encephalitis is a swelling of the brain, and it can cause brain damage. This information scares Emma and her mother, but the doctor reassures them that less than one percent of people with the West Nile virus develop West Nile encephalitis. In addition, people under the age of fifty are much less likely to get worse.

Luckily, Emma's symptoms do not get any worse, and in a few days she starts to feel a lot better. Her headache goes away, and her temperature returns to normal. She is healthy again— just in time to start the new school year. The doctor tells her that being infected with the West Nile virus might make her **immune** to it in the future. Even so, Emma vows that the next time she plays outside she will not forget the insect repellent!

2

WHAT IS A MOSQUITO-BORNE ILLNESS?

The West Nile virus is just one of the **microorganisms** (also called microbes) that mosquitoes can carry and transfer to humans. Microorganisms are tiny creatures that are too small to be seen without a microscope. Microbes that cause illnesses are also called **pathogens,** or germs.

MOSQUITOES

There are 3,500 species (types) of mosquitoes in the world. Even though they are annoying, most of these mosquitoes are harmless to humans and animals. However, there are a few species of mosquitoes that carry diseases and can pass these diseases on to animals, including humans. Organisms, such as mosquitoes, that carry and pass on diseases are called **vectors**.

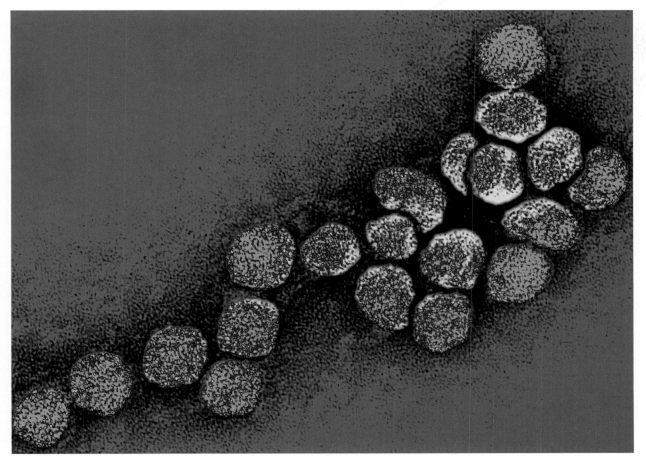

The West Nile virus, as seen under a microscope.

Not all mosquitoes are vectors. Only those that bite can pass on germs. Only female mosquitoes bite, and they only suck blood when they are almost ready to lay eggs. This is because female mosquitoes need a protein found in blood in order for their eggs to form properly. In fact, mosquitoes never drink blood as a regular meal. Instead, they drink nectar from flowers.

Both males and females have a very long mouth part called a **proboscis**. But only a female mosquito's proboscis is thin and sharp enough to get under an animal's skin. Male mosquitoes can use their proboscises only to get to the nectar deep inside a flower.

Most people cannot tell that a mosquito is biting them until it is too late. This is because mosquito saliva contains an **anesthetic**. Anesthetics are substances that stop or dull the

A mosquito pierces the skin of its victim with its sharp proboscis.

feeling of pain. A mosquito's saliva also contains an **anticoagulant**. Anticoagulants keep blood from clotting, or clumping, together. This keeps the blood flowing until the mosquito drinks her fill. When a mosquito bites and injects her saliva under the skin, the body's immune system notices that foreign substances have entered the body. Special cells in the immune system are sent to the bite to fight the invasion. This fight causes the familiar swelling, redness, and itching that we associate with a mosquito bite.

LIFE STAGES OF A MOSQUITO

Mosquitoes can be found in most parts of the world, including very cold Arctic regions. Because they live part of their lives in water, however, they are rarely found in deserts. Some types of mosquitoes lay their eggs in permanent freshwater, such as lakes or ponds. Others lay their eggs in standing water that has collected in tree stumps, buckets of rainwater, old tires, or swimming pools. Yet other mosquitoes lay their eggs in areas where the water from yearly floods will eventually cover them. Mosquitoes that live in Arctic regions lay their eggs in the snow. The eggs hatch when the snow melts. No matter where mosquitoes live, water is necessary for their life cycle.

Depending on the species, female mosquitoes can lay between fifty and three hundred eggs at one time. As an adult, a female mosquito might lay as many as a thousand eggs every

How Do the Bloodsuckers Find You?

Do you ever wonder why some people seem to get more mosquito bites than other people? Here are a few ways that female mosquitoes find their targets:

- **They can see you.** Scientists think that mosquitoes cannot see all that well, but they can see well enough—especially if someone is moving around or wearing clothing that contrasts with the background (for example, a dark shirt against a light background).
- **They can feel you.** If they get close enough, mosquitoes can feel the heat given off by mammals and birds.
- **They can smell you.** Mosquitoes can detect some gases, such as carbon dioxide. Carbon dioxide comes out of the body as a natural part of breathing. Some people breathe out more carbon dioxide than others, so they get bitten more. Mosquitoes also seem to be attracted to certain chemicals in human sweat. And, again, some people give off more of these chemicals than others. This explains why some people seem to attract, and get bitten by, more mosquitoes than other people.

Mosquitos know when you are near them because they can see you, feel you, and smell you.

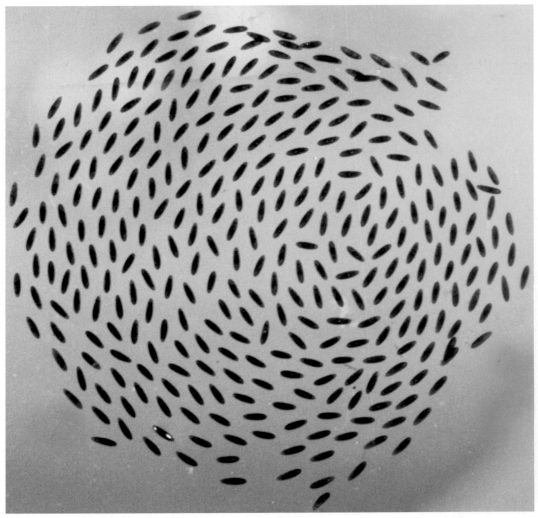

Mosquito eggs on the surface of a body of water.

year. In some species, the mosquito lays eggs on top of the water one at a time. In other species, females lay groups of one hundred to three hundred eggs together. These groups of eggs, called egg rafts, float on the surface of the water.

A few days after being laid, the eggs hatch. The wormlike creatures that emerge are called **larvae**. Mosquito larvae are also called wrigglers because of the way they move.

Mosquito larvae live near the surface of the water and breathe air through a breathing tube at the base of their tails. Depending on the mosquito species and the water temperature, the larval stage can last from a few days to several weeks.

After shedding their skin several times and growing larger, the larvae change into **pupae**. Pupae are called tumblers. Depending on the species and the water

Mosquito larvae hang from the surface of the water on which they were born.

temperature, this stage of development lasts one to four days. Both the larval and the pupal stages of the mosquito's life cycle are spent entirely in the water.

When a pupa is mature, its skin splits and an adult mosquito emerges. After climbing out of the casing that was around it, the adult mosquito must rest and spread its wings so that they can dry. They can only do this by standing on the surface of the water. This is why female mosquitoes do not lay their eggs in rapidly moving streams or fountains. When its wings are completely dry, the mosquito can fly away. It will live the rest of its life on land.

Several days after emerging from the water, adult females are ready to seek their first blood meal and to start laying eggs. Female mosquitoes can live a month or longer, but the life span of a male mosquito is only about a week.

MOSQUITO-BORNE ILLNESSES

In the majority of the United States, mosquitoes are most active between the months of June and September, when the weather is at its warmest. Therefore, most people who became infected with a mosquito-borne illness are infected during these months. However, in warmer climates, such as the southern United States and the tropical and subtropical regions of the world, mosquitoes—and the diseases they spread—can be a problem year-round.

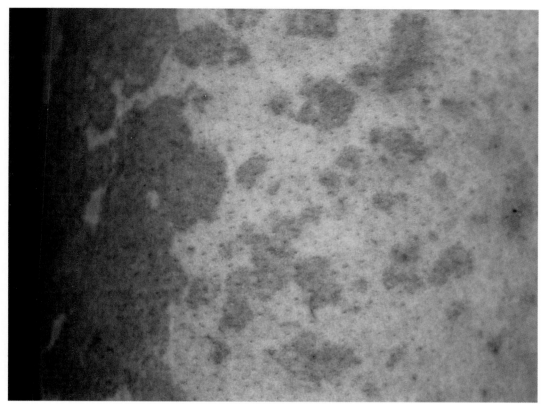

This rash is on the leg of a woman who has the West Nile virus.

The West Nile virus (WNV) is only one of the pathogens that mosquitoes can carry. Any disease caused by the bite of a mosquito is called a mosquito-borne illness. The West Nile virus, for example, finds its way into a mosquito when the mosquito bites a bird that is carrying the virus. The virus then moves to the mosquito's salivary glands and can be transmitted to any animal that the mosquito bites. Scientists have found more than 150 types of birds that can carry WNV.

Encephalitis

The West Nile virus is not the only mosquito-borne virus that can cause encephalitis in humans. Eastern equine encephalitis (EEE), Western equine encephalitis (WEE), St. Louis encephalitis (SLE), and La Crosse encephalitis (LCE) are other viral illnesses that mosquitoes can spread to humans. Like the WNV, these illnesses can cause swelling of the brain.

Of the five types of encephalitis, EEE is the most serious. It is also the rarest. On average, there are only about five cases of EEE diagnosed in the United States every year. However, about 33 percent of the patients who develop encephalitis after being infected with the virus end up dying of the disease. EEE can affect birds, horses, and humans. Like WNV, the EEE virus is transmitted from an infected bird to a human by a mosquito. A major outbreak of EEE along the East Coast of the United States in 1933 gave the disease its name. WEE is very similar to EEE, but it occurs in the western part of the United States.

St. Louis encephalitis is one of the most common mosquito-borne illnesses found in the United States. Even though the disease is named for St. Louis, Missouri, Missouri is not the only U.S. state where the disease occurs. In fact, all forty-eight mainland states, as well as parts of Canada, the Caribbean, and South America, have reported cases of SLE. Between 1964 and 2005, more than 4,500 people were diagnosed with SLE, many of them in the central and eastern states. In southern states, people can get SLE year-round. As with WNV and EEE, a mosquito can give people SLE after it bites an infected bird.

The most common form of mosquito-borne encephalitis in children under the age of sixteen is LCE. About seventy cases of LCE are reported in the United States each year. At one time, this disease was mainly found in the Great Lakes region, but recently southeastern states (West Virginia, North Carolina, Tennessee, and Virginia) have also reported cases.

Viruses that cause encephalitis do something that other viruses and bacteria cannot do. They can cross the **blood-brain barrier.** The blood-brain barrier is a layer of cells and blood vessels that normally keeps certain substances—including some medications and pathogens—from reaching the brain.

Yellow Fever

Yellow fever is another mosquito-borne illness caused by a virus. Mosquitoes get the virus by biting nonhuman primates such as monkeys. Most cases of yellow fever occur in Africa and South America. The disease is very rare in the United States today, but that has not always been the case. Occasionally, American travelers still get infected with the virus while traveling to the tropics of Africa or South America. However, there is a vaccine that can protect people from getting infected with the yellow fever virus. The immunity from the vaccine lasts for up to ten

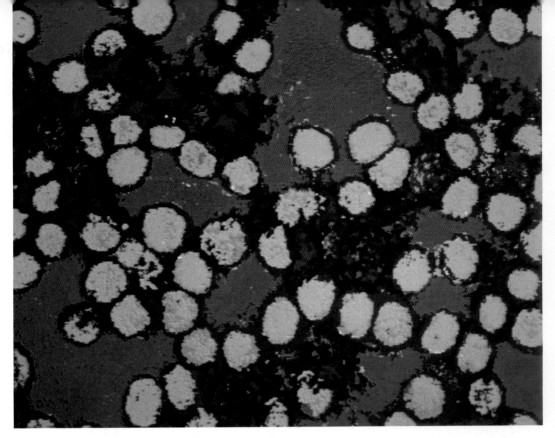
Yellow fever as seen under a microscope.

years. Doctors recommend the vaccine to people traveling to or living in areas where yellow fever still occurs.

Dengue Fever

Two other mosquito-borne illnesses are dengue fever (DF) and dengue hemorrhagic fever (DHF). Four types of viruses can cause these diseases: DEN-1, DEN-2, DEN-3, and DEN-4. If a person gets one of the viruses, he or she is immune to that type. These viruses can be spread only when a mosquito bites an infected person and then bites someone else. They cannot be spread from human to human through bodily contact.

The same four viruses cause both DF and DHF. However, DHF is a much more serious disease than DF. People who have previously been infected with another type of DF virus, people with weak immune systems, and older people seem to be more at risk of developing the more severe DHF.

Many people who live in tropical or subtropical regions are at risk of developing DF or DHF. Worldwide, about 50 million to 100 million people get DF, and several hundred thousand people develop DHF every year. Occasionally people report cases in the United States and its territories. Most of these cases occur in Texas and Puerto Rico.

Malaria

Viruses are not the only germs that mosquitoes can carry. They can carry tiny organisms called parasites, too. Four different types of single-celled *Plasmodium* parasites can cause malaria in humans: falciparum, malariae, ovale, and vivax. Of these four parasites, *Plasmodium falciparum* is the most common. This parasite also causes the most severe symptoms and the highest number of malaria deaths every year.

A female mosquito picks up *Plasmodium* parasites by biting an infected human. The parasite reproduces inside her and moves to her salivary glands. When the mosquito bites another human, the parasite is passed on to that victim through her saliva. The ability of a mosquito species to transfer the malaria

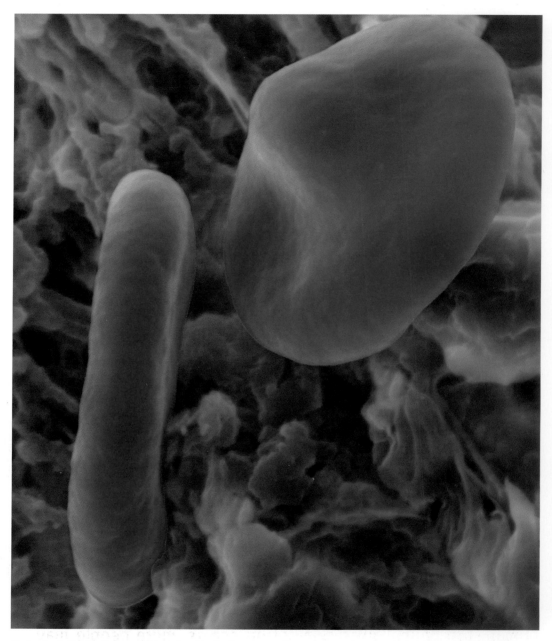

Malaria infects the red blood cells in humans. Seen here, a normal red blood cell (left) and an infected one (right).

parasite to humans depends on two things: the life span of the mosquito and the temperature. It takes about ten to eighteen days for the parasite to complete its cycle in the mosquito host. If the mosquito dies before the cycle is complete, the parasite dies with it. Higher temperatures allow the parasites to mature faster, and more mature parasites are more likely to infect a human host than younger ones.

Once the parasite is in the human body, it starts to grow and divide. It does this first in the person's liver. When liver cells contain too many parasites, they burst and release the parasites into the person's bloodstream. There they continue to grow, to divide, and to start causing the symptoms of malaria.

Without treatment, malaria can lead to death. Every year, 300 million to 500 million people worldwide get malaria. And the disease kills more than one million of them, mostly children living in sub-Saharan Africa (the area of Africa below the Sahara Desert). Malaria is very rare in the United States today, but it is still a large problem in other parts of the world, such as Africa, Asia, the Middle East, and Central and South America. Almost 90 percent of malaria cases occur in Africa. Even though the disease is limited to certain regions, some scientists are concerned that, due to climate change, mosquitoes currently living, these regions may be able to expand their living area. If this shift in mosquito population occurs, more people may be infected with mosquito-borne illnesses such as malaria.

3

THE HISTORY OF MOSQUITO-BORNE ILLNESSES

Although there are still many things to learn about mosquito-borne illnesses, scientists today know a lot about them. This was not always the case, however. It was not until the late nineteenth century that scientists began to suspect that insects could give diseases to humans. The first scientist to prove this link was Patrick Manson, a British doctor. In 1878, Manson traced a disease called elephantiasis to a parasite carried by a mosquito. If mosquitoes could carry one disease, he reasoned, they could probably carry others, too.

THE HISTORY OF MALARIA

In 1894, Manson suggested to Ronald Ross, a British scientist working on the malaria problem in India, that mosquitoes might be the missing link between parasite and human in malaria cases. Based on research carried out in 1880 by a French army surgeon named Charles Louis Alphonse Laveran, Ross knew that malaria was caused by pro-tozoa—tiny, single-celled, animal-like creatures. Laveran proved that all malaria patients had these parasites in their blood, but he did not know how they got there.

After discussing the problem with Manson, Ross figured out that mosquitoes were likely transferring the parasite from one person to the next. To test his theory,

In the late 1800s, Ronald Ross worked on finding a link between parasites and malaria.

Ross continued his research with malaria-infected birds. He learned not only that the malaria parasite could be transferred from bird to mosquito, but also that the mosquito could trans-fer the parasite to a bird that was not infected. This discovery proved that mosquitoes were the link needed to transmit the disease. Both Ross and Laveran were awarded Nobel Prizes for their work. Ross received his prize in 1902, and Laveran claimed his in 1907.

Malaria has plagued humans for a very long time. In October 2008, scientists discovered the oldest evidence of the *Plasmodium falciparum* parasite in several Egyptian mummies. These mummies died between 3,500 BCE and 500 BCE. Before the discovery of these mummies, the oldest known evidence of the disease was in the written records of Greek physician Hippocrates. Hippocrates described malaria in 400 BCE.

Hippocrates's recordings of malaria were not the first written record of the disease, however. In fact, as far back as 2700 BCE, ancient Chinese medical writing described the symptoms of malaria. The first treatment for malaria was also recorded by the Chinese. In the year 340 BCE, Ge Hong of the East Yin Dynasty reported that the Qinghao plant (called sweet wormwood in the United States) could help reduce a fever caused by malaria. In 1971, Chinese scientists identified the active ingredient in the plant. This active ingredient is still used today in antimalarial medications.

In the early seventeenth century, another effective treatment for malaria was discovered in Peru. Monks in the area found that a drink made from the bark of the cinchona tree could reduce malarial fevers. The cinchona tree lives in the rain forests of the Andes Mountains in South America. In 1820, French scientists Pierre-Joseph Pelletier and Joseph Bienaimé

A chemical in the bark of the cinchona tree helps relieve the symptoms of malaria.

Caventou found the active chemical in the cinchona tree's bark. They named the chemical quinine.

When the monks brought this malaria treatment back to Europe, demand for the bark of the cinchona tree grew quickly. People destroyed many trees in an effort to harvest the bark. By the mid-1800s, the trees became harder to find in their native Peru. However, people had exported seeds of the cinchona tree to other areas of the world, against the wishes of the Peruvian government. By the late 1800s, a grove of cinchona trees had been established on the Indonesian island of Java. This crop of trees eventually supplied almost 80 percent of the world's supply of quinine.

During World War I, however, Java was captured and the quinine supply was cut off. Desperately searching for a way to protect their troops fighting in eastern Africa from being wiped out by malaria, German scientists began to experiment with ways to make a synthetic (man-made) version of quinine. In 1934, Hans Andersag, a German chemist, successfully made the antimalaria drug chloroquine.

Chloroquine pills are a man-made treatment for the symptoms of malaria.

For a time, chloroquine and an insecticide (a chemical that kills insects) called DDT were the main weapons scientists used to fight malaria. However, after about a decade of use, the malaria parasite began to show **resistance** to chloroquine. This means the parasite had changed over time so that chloroquine no longer harmed it. Because of this resistance, doctors are again prescribing quinine to control the parasite in some malaria cases today.

Both quinine and its synthetic counterpart, chloroquine, fight malaria by preventing the parasite from reproducing. DDT,

Mosquitoes and the Food Chain

As annoying as mosquitoes are to humans, these insects are a good source of food for many animals. Geckoes, birds, frogs, and bats all feed on adult mosquitoes. Water striders, dragonflies, and fish find mosquito larvae a tasty meal. Because they feed on nectar, adult mosquitoes help pollinate flowers by carrying pollen from one flower to another.

on the other hand, controls the disease by killing the vectors—the mosquitoes that can carry the parasite. DDT played a role in eliminating malaria from the United States. Beginning in the summer of 1947, state and local health agencies in thirteen southeastern states began to spray DDT in areas where malaria was a problem. Fifteen thousand malaria cases had been reported in America that year. By the end of 1949, more than 4.6 million homes had been treated with the pesticide. In 1950, only two thousand cases of malaria were reported in the United States. And by 1951, U.S. officials no longer considered malaria

DDT was sprayed from planes in the 1940s in order to kill mosquito populations that carried malaria.

to be a major health threat to the nation. In the 1970s, however, scientific research showed that DDT harms the environment, and the insecticide has been banned in the United States for more than thirty years. Today, different insecticides are used to control the mosquito populations in high-risk areas.

Even though malaria nearly disappeared from the United States in the early 1950s, the disease still appears every now and then. In 2002, for example, more than a thousand Americans were diagnosed with the disease. Eight of those people died. Scientists determined that all but five of the victims had visited countries where malaria is prevalent. The other five must have contracted malaria after a mosquito in the United States bit one of the infected travelers and passed on the parasite. Between 1953 and 2003, sixty-three cases of malaria were passed from one American to another in this manner.

THE HISTORY OF YELLOW FEVER

As with malaria, outbreaks of yellow fever have been reported throughout history. But it was not until an outbreak among U.S. soldiers stationed in Havana, Cuba, during the Spanish-American War in 1898 that American scientists started trying to find out how the disease was spread. More than fifty years earlier, a Cuban physician named Carlos Finlay suggested that insects were spreading the disease. In 1900, following up on

Netting over a bed, like the one seen here, is used in many countries to keep mosquitoes away from people as they sleep.

Finlay's suggestion, physician Walter Reed, along with other scientists of the U.S. Army Yellow Fever Commission, proved that mosquitoes did indeed transmit yellow fever. After this discovery, yellow fever victims slept behind mosquito screens and possible mosquito breeding areas were destroyed. No further outbreaks occurred in Havana.

The last major yellow fever outbreak in the United States was in New Orleans in 1905. There are still a few cases here and there, though. Between 1996 and 2002, yellow fever caused three deaths in the United States. Doctors determined that all three patients caught the illness during a visit to South America.

THE HISTORY OF DENGUE FEVER

In 1779, the first large outbreak of dengue fever (DF) was reported in Africa, Asia, and North America. The more serious form of the disease, dengue hemorrhagic fever (DHF), did not emerge until the 1950s, when there was a major outbreak in the Philippines and Thailand. Since that time, mosquitoes that carry the virus that causes both diseases have been found in tropical areas all over the world, including some areas in the United States. In 2001, more than a thousand Hawaiians were hospitalized with DF. In 2005, twenty-four people in Brownsville, Texas, came down with the disease. Luckily, none of the patients developed DHF.

A Virus That Mosquitoes
Cannot Carry

Mosquitoes can transmit some terrible diseases, but one virus that they cannot carry is the human immunodeficiency virus (HIV). HIV is the virus that causes acquired immunodeficiency syndrome (AIDS). HIV cannot live inside mosquitoes. Therefore, even if a mosquito bites someone who is infected with HIV, the virus cannot be passed from one person to another through a mosquito bite.

THE HISTORY OF MOSQUITO-BORNE ENCEPHALITIS

In August 1999, New York City was the first place in the United States to report the emergence of the West Nile virus. Since that time, approximately 16,000 Americans have become ill after being infected with the WNV and more than 6,000 have died. Every state except Alaska and Hawaii has reported cases of the disease. However, many more Americans have probably been infected with the virus and are now immune to it. This is because about 80 percent of people who are infected with the WNV never know that they have it because they do not have any symptoms.

The West Nile virus may not have shown up in the United States until 1999, but it is hardly a new disease. The first known case was diagnosed in Uganda, Africa, in 1937. The virus was reported in Europe and the Middle East long before it was found in America. Scientists are not certain how the virus made the leap from Africa, Europe, or the Middle East to the United States. They believe that someone traveled to a place where the WNV is common, was infected while abroad, and unknowingly brought the virus back with them.

Since 1831, long before the WNV was a problem in the United States, the Eastern equine encephalitis (EEE) virus has been causing illness in North American horses. However, it was not until a major outbreak occurred in horses along the East

A laboratory tests mosquitoes for the West Nile virus in June 2003, when there was an outbreak of close to nine hundred cases of the disease it causes.

Coast in 1933 that the disease got its name. The following year, scientists determined that EEE was a mosquito-borne disease. In 1935, scientists suggested that birds might also be able to carry the virus, an idea that was proven correct in 1950.

The first human case of EEE was reported in 1938. On average, there are only about twelve to seventeen cases of the disease reported in humans in the United States each year. But some years can be worse than others. In 2003, for example, North Carolina reported an outbreak of twenty-six cases of EEE.

Other types of mosquito-borne viral encephalitis have been named for the places where they were first recognized. St. Louis encephalitis, for example, was diagnosed for the first time in St. Louis, Missouri, in 1933. Today, the virus is found throughout North, South, and Central America as well as the Caribbean. In the United States, major outbreaks of the disease have happened mainly in the western United States, the Mississippi Valley, along the Gulf Coast, and in Florida.

Another mosquito-borne illness named for the city in which it was discovered is La Crosse encephalitis. This disease emerged as a new mosquito-borne illness in the United States in 1963, when it was first diagnosed during an outbreak in La Crosse, Wisconsin.

4

DIAGNOSING AND TREATING A MOSQUITO-BORNE ILLNESS

While mosquito-borne illnesses are not very common in the United States, they do exist. Like the West Nile virus that infected Emma, the symptoms of many mosquito-borne illnesses mimic those of the flu virus. However, most mosquito-borne illnesses can develop into much more serious diseases. Therefore, it is good to know their signs and symptoms. If you or anyone in your family develops these symptoms, it is best to see a doctor. Only a doctor can make a proper diagnosis of what is making you sick.

HAVE YOU BEEN INFECTED?

With so many mosquitoes buzzing around in the summertime, how do you know if you have been bitten by one that carries a virus that causes illness? One thing to look for is flu-like symptoms in the summertime. Most people come down with the flu in the winter, but mosquitoes are more active—and more likely to bite people—from June to September.

If you live in one of the warmer regions of the country, mosquitoes may be active year-round, so your chances of being infected exist year-round as well. If you have flu-like symptoms at any time of year, you might want to take a trip to the doctor's office.

West Nile Virus

As Emma's doctor told her, the WNV can cause encephalitis, a swelling of the brain. It can also cause **meningitis.** Meningitis is an inflammation of the covering of the brain and spinal cord. Both encephalitis and meningitis are very serious. They can cause permanent damage to the brain or spinal cord and even death. Seek medical attention immediately if you have symptoms such as high fever, severe headache, neck stiffness, confusion, extreme sleepiness, and sensitivity to light.

Luckily, less than one percent of people infected with the WNV develop a severe illness. In fact, almost 80 percent of people bitten by a mosquito carrying the WNV have no symptoms at all. Most likely, they will never know that they have been infected.

Of the 20 percent of people who do develop symptoms, most experience only mild flu-like symptoms, such as a mild fever, headache, body aches, and nausea (feeling the urge to vomit).

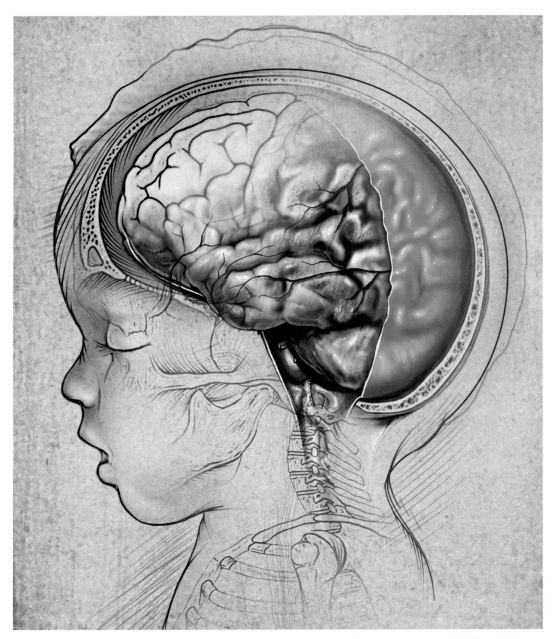

The West Nile virus can cause meningitis in some people. Meningitis is a swelling of the covering of the brain and spinal cord.

They may also have swollen lymph nodes and a rash on their chest, stomach, and back. The symptoms start to appear about three to fourteen days after the person is infected with the virus, and they usually last a couple of days.

There is no treatment for WNV. People who develop the symptoms just have to wait for the illness to go away on its own. Symptoms can be treated much like those of the flu: drink lots of fluids and get plenty of rest. Certain medications may also be used to relieve the pain of headaches, muscle aches, or back pain. Doctors recommend staying away from aspirin, however. Scientific research has shown a link between viral illnesses, the use of aspirin, and an increased risk of developing a life-threatening condition called Reye's syndrome.

Anyone who develops symptoms of encephalitis or meningitis should be hospitalized immediately. Doctors cannot cure West Nile encephalitis, but they can watch over the patient and attempt to relieve the pressure on the brain and spinal cord that results from the swelling.

Other Types of Encephalitis

Like those who are infected with WNV, people infected with La Crosse virus tend to have mild flu-like symptoms—fever, headache, a general feeling of tiredness, nausea, and vomiting. However, some people contract the more severe form of the illness. Symptoms of La Crosse encephalitis (LCE) include seizures, coma, and paralysis. They usually appear between five and fifteen days after a bite by an infected mosquito. Children under the age of sixteen are more likely to be affected by La Crosse virus than any other age group. There is no medical treatment for LCE.

The symptoms of the SLE and EEE viruses are also very similar to those of WNV. Most people infected with these viruses have no symptoms. Some people develop flu-like symptoms. A very small number of people develop encephalitis.

Also like the WNV, once a person is infected by the La Crosse, St. Louis, or Eastern equine encephalitis virus, he or she is immune to that virus. It cannot make him or her sick again. However, the person can be infected with a different virus.

Malaria

Malaria causes flu-like symptoms—fever, chills, headaches, muscle aches, and a general feeling of being ill. These symptoms usually show up about six to eight days after being infected with the parasite, but depending on the species of parasite, symptoms may not appear for a month.

Malaria symptoms differ from those of the diseases that can develop into encephalitis. Malaria symptoms often come in waves. People with malaria may feel as if they have the flu, start to feel better after a few days, and then start to feel sick all over again. This cycling in malaria patients matches the reproductive cycle of the parasites in their bodies. This pattern of symptoms helps doctors tell the difference between malaria and different mosquito-borne illness.

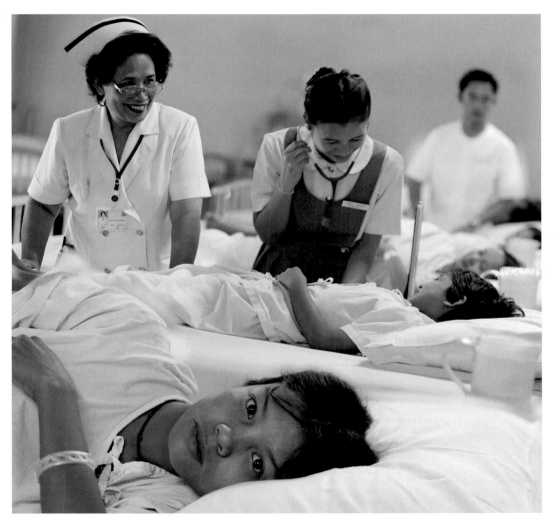

A number of patients at this hospital in Bangkok are being treated for malaria.

To be absolutely certain that a patient has malaria, laboratory blood tests are usually necessary. To do the laboratory test, scientists spread a sample of the patient's blood on a slide and treat it with a special stain. If the person is infected with malaria, the scientists can see the parasite when they look at the stained blood cells under a microscope.

Doctors can treat malaria with medication. Because the medication interrupts the parasites' reproductive cycle, it needs to be taken exactly as a doctor prescribes it in order to be effective. The same medication is also used to prevent infection by the malaria parasite in the first place. For this reason, doctors recommend that people who travel to areas where malaria is common take the medication before they leave home, during their trip, and for a few weeks after they return. If malaria is left untreated, it can be fatal.

Yellow Fever

Yellow fever is another preventable mosquito-borne illness. There is a vaccine that can prevent people from contracting the illness. Doctors recommend that travelers get vaccinated before traveling to countries where yellow fever is a problem. Once a person is infected with the yellow fever virus, doctors can treat the symptoms of the disease, but they cannot kill the virus itself. However, once a person has had yellow fever and has recovered from it, he or she cannot get the illness again.

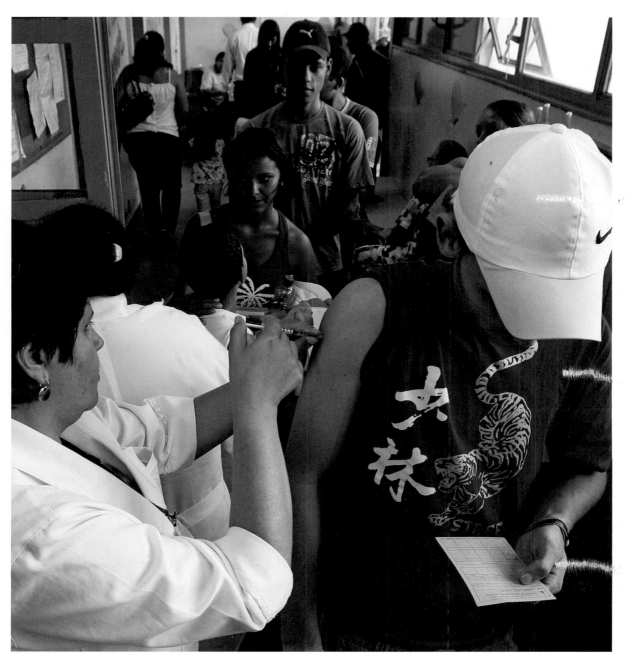

Residents of Brazilia, Brazil, line up to get immunized against yellow fever.

Like other mosquito-borne viruses, the yellow fever virus usually causes mild flu-like symptoms. The symptoms normally begin to appear about three to six days after the mosquito bite. Occasionally, however, yellow fever can become much more serious. When this occurs, the illness may seem to disappear for a period of time, but then the patient becomes ill again. When the illness returns, it may cause more severe symptoms, such as high fever, nose bleeds, bleeding gums, and severe bruising. If the illness continues, it can lead to kidney or liver failure. Liver failure can cause a build-up of a chemical called bilirubin in the blood. An accumulation of bilirubin causes the skin and the whites of the eyes to turn yellow. This condition is called **jaundice**. The yellowish tint of a yellow fever patient's skin gives the disease its name.

Dengue Fever

The symptoms of dengue fever (DF) include a sudden high fever, severe headache, and muscle and joint aches. Because of the joint pain associated with the disease, DF is sometimes called break-bone fever.

Dengue hemorrhagic fever, however, is a much more serious disease. DHF can result in uncontrollable, heavy bleeding. This condition is called **hemorrhaging**. If DHF is not diagnosed and treated quickly, it can be life threatening. There are no specific medicines for DF or DHF. However, people suffering from DHF

Mosquito-Borne Illness	Symptoms	Incubation Time
West Nile virus Eastern equine encephalitis La Crosse encephalitis St. Louis encephalitis	**mild:** fever, chills, headache, body aches, nausea, vomiting, fatigue **severe:** seizure, coma, paralysis, permanent brain damage, death	3 to 14 days (WNV) 3 to 10 days (EEE) 5 to 15 days (LCE) 5 to 15 days (SLE)
malaria	**mild:** fever, chills, headache, muscle aches, general fatigue—symptoms often appear and disappear in a cyclic fashion **severe:** can be fatal if left untreated	6 to 30 days
yellow fever	**mild:** fever, chills, severe headache, back pain, muscle aches, nausea, vomiting, fatigue, weakness **severe:** bleeding, jaundice, death	3 to 6 days
dengue fever	**mild:** high fever, severe headache, muscle and joint aches **severe:** internal bleeding, severe nosebleeds, bleeding gums, severe bruising, death	3 to 14 days

may need new blood to replace the blood that they have lost. This is done by giving the patient a **blood transfusion**.

Scientists have not yet developed a vaccine that can protect people from infection with the virus that causes DF. The best way to prevent DF and DHF is to avoid being bitten by a mosquito that might carry the viruses.

HOW TO PREVENT MOSQUITO-BORNE ILLNESSES

Mosquito bites are not always easy to prevent, but there are some ways to protect yourself. One of the best ways to stay away from mosquitoes is not to spend much time outdoors in the summertime—but that is not much fun. So when you do go outside, wear long-sleeved shirts and pants. This can help protect tender skin from the probe of the female mosquito's proboscis. Spraying insect repellent on exposed skin can also discourage the bugs from biting you. Many mosquitoes are especially active in the early morning and at dusk (although the mosquito that spreads yellow fever prefers to bite during daylight hours). Limiting your time outdoors during those hours can help reduce the risk of mosquito bites as well. Finally, wearing light-colored clothing might help. Scientists have found that mosquitoes seem to be more attracted to dark colors.

The Centers for Disease Control (CDC) recommends that children use insect repellents that contain up to 10 percent DEET. Adults can use repellents that contain and up to 30 percent

One way to avoid getting bitten by a mosquito is to use insect repellent.

Mosquitoes and Your Family Pet

....

Your family pet is not immune to mosquito-borne illnesses, but pets get a different illness. Instead of spreading malaria or WNV, mosquitoes can infect dogs and cats with heartworms.

Heartworms are large worms that can live in the heart. Dogs are the most common hosts, but cats, ferrets, foxes, wolves, and horses can also be infected with these parasites. Fully grown, these spaghetti-like worms can be 10 to 12 inches (25 to 30 centimeters) long. If left untreated, heartworms can block arteries (blood vessels) in the heart and eventually cause heart failure and death.

A birdbath is one place where mosquito larvae can live. To avoid accidentally breeding mosquitoes, you should change the water in your birdbath at least once a week.

DEET. The higher the percentage of DEET in an insect repellent, the longer the repellent will work against mosquitoes. The CDC also recommends making sure that window screens in your home are not torn. Window screens prevent mosquitoes from entering homes. Finally, if you plan a trip away from home, check with the CDC to see if mosquito-borne illnesses are a problem in the area where you will be traveling. If they are, be sure to arrange to get the proper medication or vaccinations before you go.

Another way to prevent mosquito-borne illnesses is to control the population of mosquitoes. To decrease the number of mosquitoes, some communities spray insecticides that kill adult mosquitoes and larvae. However, communities must strike a fine balance between eliminating the mosquito population and spraying pesticides that might make people sick.

Getting rid of standing water can also reduce the mosquito population. If there is no standing water, mosquitoes cannot breed. Standing water often accumulates in unused swimming pools, buckets that have collected rainwater, and old tires. Birdbaths can also make good breeding grounds for mosquitoes if the water is not changed about once a week. Also make sure to change the water in your pet's outdoor water bowl every day.

The best ways to prevent the spread of mosquito-borne illnesses are to cover up, to use insect repellent, to stay inside at dawn and dusk, and to get rid of standing water where female mosquitoes can lay their eggs. By taking these steps in advance, we can all continue to enjoy our summer cookouts and activities without the fear of infection.

GLOSSARY

anesthetic—A substance that reduces or stops pain.

anticoagulant—A substance that prevents blood from clotting.

bacteria—A tiny, one-celled living thing that reproduces by dividing.

blood-brain barrier—A barrier that prevents some substances from entering the brain.

blood transfusion—The replacement of lost blood with blood donated by someone else.

contagious—Able to be passed from person to person.

encephalitis—Swelling of the brain.

hemorrhaging—The loss of blood through uncontrollable, heavy bleeding.

immune—Protected from a disease.

immune system—The body's defense system against germs that can cause disease.

jaundice—A disease caused by the buildup of bilirubin in the blood, which causes the skin and the whites of the eyes to turn yellowish.

larvae—Animals that make up the first step in an insect's life cycle.

lymph nodes—Small glands that are a part of the immune system and are found throughout the body.

meningitis—An inflammation of the covering of the brain and spinal cord.

microorganisms (microbes)—Tiny life forms such as viruses, bacteria, and protozoa.

parasite—An organism living in, with, or on another organism.

pathogens—Organisms that can cause disease.

proboscis—The long, thin mouthpart that a mosquito uses to drink blood or nectar.

pupae—Animals that make up the second step in an insect's life cycle.

resistance—The ability to change over time so that drugs that once worked do not work anymore.

symptom—Something that indicates the existence of something else.

vectors—Organisms that can carry and pass on a disease.

viruses—A microorganism smaller than bacteria that can only divide and grow inside a living organism.

FIND OUT MORE

Organizations

Centers for Disease Control (CDC)
1600 Clifton Road
Atlanta, GA 30333
1-800-232-4636
www.cdc.gov/

World Health Organization (WHO)
20 Avenue Appia
1211 Geneva 27
Switzerland
www.who.int/malaria/

Books

Barnard, Bryn. *Outbreak! Plagues That Changed History*. New York: Random House, 2005.

Loewen, Nancy. *Bzzz, Bzzz!: Mosquitoes in Your Backyard*. Mankato, MN: Capstone Press Inc., 2005.

Markle, Sandra. *Mosquitoes: Tiny Insect Troublemakers*. Minneapolis, MN: Lerner Publishing Group, 2008.

Siy, Alexandra. *Mosquito Bite*. Watertown, MA: Charlesbridge Publishing Inc., 2005.

Snedden, Robert. *Fighting Infectious Diseases*. Chicago: Heinemann, 2007.

Wyborny, Sheila. *The Malaria Parasite*. Detroit, MI: Gale, Cengage Learning, 2005.

Web Sites

KidsHealth
http://kidshealth.org/kid/ill_injure/bugs/mosquito.html

ScienceNews for Kids
http://www.sciencenewsforkids.org/articles/20040811/Feature1.asp

The Why Files
http://whyfiles.org/016skeeter/

Neuroscience for Kids
http://faculty.washington.edu/chudler/deeta.html

Mosquito Life Cycle
http://www.ct.gov/DEP/cwp/view.asp?a=2723&q=326190&depNav_GID=1655

INDEX

Page numbers for illustrations are in **boldface**.

ABOUT THE AUTHOR

Kristi Lew is the author of more than twenty science books for teachers and young people. Fascinated with science from a young age, she studied biochemistry and genetics in college. Before she started writing full-time, she worked in genetic laboratories for more than ten years and taught high-school science. When she's not writing, she enjoys sailing with her husband aboard their small sailboat, *Proton*. She lives, writes, sails, and uses lots of insect repellent in St. Petersburg, Florida.